This book belongs to

_____

This book is dedicated to my children - Mikey, Kobe, and Jojo.

Copyright © 2025 by Grow Grit Press LLC. All rights reserved. No part of this book may be reproduced in any form without permission in writing from the publisher. Please send bulk order requests to growgritpress@gmail.com Printed and bound in the USA. MiniMovers.tv
Paperback ISBN: 979-8-89614-103-7 Hardcover ISBN: 979-8-89614-105-1

Sophie Cruz

By Mary Nhin

Hi, I'm Sophie Cruz, and when I was five years old, I had a big worry.

I loved playing with my little sister, riding my bike, and helping Mamá make warm tortillas in the kitchen. But every night, as I lay in bed, I had the same fear—what if my parents were taken away?

Mamá and Papá came from Mexico to build a better life for us. But because they didn't have papers, they could be sent back at any time. That meant I might wake up one day, and they'd be gone.

I didn't think it was fair. Families should stay together.

Then one day, I learned about the Pope, a leader who cared about helping people. He was coming to Washington, D.C. to speak in front of thousands. I had an idea—what if I gave him a letter asking him to help?

When I told Mamá and Papá my plan, they sighed.
"*Mi amor, you are just a little girl,*" Mamá said.
"*No one will listen to you,*" Papá added.

But I didn't believe that.
"*If I don't speak up, who will?*" I asked.

So we traveled to Washington, D.C. with other families like mine. The streets were crowded with people. The Pope rode by in his car, waving. I ran past the crowd, holding my letter tight.

The guards saw me. The people gasped.
Would they stop me?
Then, the Pope looked my way.
He waved me forward.

My heart pounded as I handed him my letter. In it, I had drawn a family—my family—with a message written in bright crayon:

"Please don't take my parents away. Families belong together."

That moment changed everything.

People started listening. Reporters wanted to talk to me. Leaders started discussing ways to protect families like mine. I was invited to march in protests, speak in front of thousands, and even visit the Supreme Court—where big decisions are made.

I stood on a stage, microphone in hand, looking at a sea of faces. My voice shook, but I spoke anyway:
"I am not afraid. I am not afraid because love is stronger than fear."

And guess what? The world listened.

I met presidents. I spoke at rallies. I helped pass laws that protected immigrant families. And I kept reminding people—even the smallest voices can make the biggest difference.

Now, I continue to fight for families. I tell children like me:

"You are never too young to stand up for what is right. Your voice matters. You matter."

Because when you speak from the heart, you can change the world.

Today, I still advocate for a just society. From everything that I have accomplished, I hope to inspire others to stand up for equity and try to make a positive change.

After my letter to the Pope, I became a voice for immigrant families everywhere.

- I spoke at the Women's March in front of thousands.
- I met President Obama and other leaders to talk about immigration.
- I helped bring awareness to DACA, a program that protects young immigrants.
- I traveled across the country, telling kids like me to be brave and never stay silent.

Today, I am still fighting for families. I dream of a future where no child has to fear losing their parents. And I believe, with all my heart—that future is possible.

No matter who you are or where you come from, you can stand up for equity and change the world.

Timeline

2010 – Sophie was born in Los Angeles, California, to undocumented immigrant parents from Oaxaca, Mexico

2015 – Sophie met with the Pope for the first time at the age of 5

2016 – Sophie starred in "Free like the Birds" and speaks at the Women's March at the age of 6

2017 – Sophie meets President Obama and visits the Supreme Court

minimovers.tv

 @marynhin   @officialninjalifehacks
#minimoversandshakers

 Ninja Life Hacks

 Mary Nhin   Ninja Life Hacks

 @officialninjalifehacks

www.ingramcontent.com/pod-product-compliance
Lightning Source LLC
LaVergne TN
LVHW070436070526
838199LV00015B/523